50 Simple and Elegant Dinner Party Recipes

By: Kelly Johnson

Table of Contents

- Lemon Garlic Shrimp Scampi
- Beef Wellington Bites
- Grilled Salmon with Dill and Lemon
- Roasted Butternut Squash Soup
- Caprese Salad with Balsamic Glaze
- Herb-Crusted Lamb Chops
- Stuffed Mushrooms with Cream Cheese and Herbs
- Spinach and Ricotta Stuffed Chicken Breast
- Seared Scallops with Citrus Butter Sauce
- Roasted Vegetable Medley
- Prosciutto-Wrapped Asparagus
- Classic Caesar Salad
- Chicken Piccata with Capers
- Roasted Potatoes with Rosemary and Garlic
- Duck Breast with Red Wine Reduction
- Mushroom Risotto
- Seared Tuna with Soy-Maple Glaze
- Roasted Beet and Goat Cheese Salad
- Lobster Bisque
- Parmesan Crusted Tilapia
- Honey-Glazed Carrots with Thyme
- Filet Mignon with Garlic Butter
- Grilled Vegetables with Balsamic Glaze
- Creamy Polenta with Wild Mushrooms
- Shrimp and Grits
- Grilled Rack of Lamb with Mint Yogurt Sauce
- Crab Cakes with Lemon Aioli
- Roasted Cauliflower with Tahini Sauce
- Braised Short Ribs with Mashed Potatoes
- Lemon Herb Roasted Chicken
- Ratatouille
- Seared Duck Breast with Cherry Sauce
- Spaghetti Aglio e Olio
- Pan-Seared Chicken Thighs with Lemon-Thyme Sauce
- Grilled Swordfish with Mango Salsa

- Eggplant Parmesan
- Stuffed Bell Peppers with Quinoa and Feta
- Grilled Pork Tenderloin with Apple Chutney
- Spinach Salad with Berries and Walnuts
- Braised Lamb Shank with Garlic Mashed Potatoes
- Grilled Vegetable and Halloumi Skewers
- Pan-Seared Sea Bass with Lemon Caper Sauce
- Pappardelle with Wild Mushrooms
- Roasted Herb-Butter Cornish Hen
- Beetroot Salad with Arugula and Walnuts
- Shrimp and Avocado Salad
- Baked Ziti with Fresh Mozzarella
- Grilled Flatbreads with Olive Tapenade
- Sweet Potato Gnocchi with Sage Butter
- Tiramisu with Fresh Berries

Lemon Garlic Shrimp Scampi

Ingredients:

- 1 lb large shrimp, peeled and deveined
- 3 tablespoons butter
- 2 tablespoons olive oil
- 5 cloves garlic, minced
- 1/4 teaspoon red pepper flakes (optional)
- Juice and zest of 1 lemon
- 1/2 cup dry white wine
- Salt and pepper to taste
- 1/4 cup fresh parsley, chopped
- 1 lb spaghetti or pasta of choice

Instructions:

1. Cook the pasta according to package instructions, then drain and set aside.
2. In a large skillet, heat the butter and olive oil over medium-high heat. Add the garlic and red pepper flakes (if using), and sauté for 1-2 minutes until fragrant.
3. Add the shrimp and cook for 2-3 minutes on each side, or until pink and cooked through.
4. Add the lemon juice, zest, and white wine to the skillet, and bring to a simmer. Let cook for 2-3 minutes.
5. Season with salt and pepper to taste.
6. Toss the cooked pasta with the shrimp and sauce. Garnish with fresh parsley and serve.

Beef Wellington Bites

Ingredients:

- 1 lb beef tenderloin, cut into bite-sized cubes
- 2 tablespoons olive oil
- Salt and pepper to taste
- 1/2 cup Dijon mustard
- 1 sheet puff pastry, thawed
- 1/4 cup mushrooms, finely chopped
- 1/4 cup pâté (optional)
- 1 egg, beaten for egg wash

Instructions:

1. Preheat the oven to 400°F (200°C).
2. Heat olive oil in a skillet over high heat. Sear the beef cubes for 1-2 minutes on each side, until browned. Remove from the heat and let cool.
3. Brush each beef cube with Dijon mustard.
4. Roll out the puff pastry and cut into small squares large enough to wrap each beef cube.
5. Place a small spoonful of mushrooms and pâté (if using) in the center of each pastry square, then place the beef cube on top.
6. Fold the pastry around the beef and seal the edges.
7. Brush each wrapped beef bite with the beaten egg.
8. Place the bites on a baking sheet and bake for 12-15 minutes, or until the pastry is golden brown. Serve warm.

Grilled Salmon with Dill and Lemon

Ingredients:

- 4 salmon fillets
- 2 tablespoons olive oil
- Salt and pepper to taste
- 2 tablespoons fresh dill, chopped
- Juice and zest of 1 lemon
- 1 lemon, sliced for garnish

Instructions:

1. Preheat the grill to medium-high heat.
2. Brush the salmon fillets with olive oil and season with salt and pepper.
3. Grill the salmon for 4-5 minutes per side, or until it flakes easily with a fork.
4. In a small bowl, combine the fresh dill, lemon juice, and zest.
5. Once the salmon is cooked, drizzle the dill and lemon mixture over the fillets.
6. Garnish with lemon slices and serve.

Roasted Butternut Squash Soup

Ingredients:

- 1 medium butternut squash, peeled, seeded, and cubed
- 1 tablespoon olive oil
- Salt and pepper to taste
- 1 medium onion, chopped
- 2 cloves garlic, minced
- 4 cups vegetable broth
- 1/2 cup heavy cream (optional)
- 1/2 teaspoon ground nutmeg

Instructions:

1. Preheat the oven to 400°F (200°C).
2. Toss the cubed butternut squash with olive oil, salt, and pepper. Spread it in a single layer on a baking sheet.
3. Roast for 25-30 minutes, or until the squash is tender and caramelized.
4. In a large pot, heat a little olive oil and sauté the onion and garlic until softened, about 5 minutes.
5. Add the roasted squash to the pot with vegetable broth. Bring to a boil, then reduce to a simmer and cook for 10-15 minutes.
6. Use an immersion blender to puree the soup until smooth.
7. Stir in the heavy cream (if using) and ground nutmeg. Season with salt and pepper to taste.
8. Serve hot, garnished with a dollop of cream if desired.

Caprese Salad with Balsamic Glaze

Ingredients:

- 4 large tomatoes, sliced
- 1 ball fresh mozzarella, sliced
- 1/4 cup fresh basil leaves
- 1/4 cup balsamic glaze
- Salt and pepper to taste

Instructions:

1. Arrange the tomato and mozzarella slices alternately on a platter.
2. Tuck fresh basil leaves between the slices.
3. Drizzle with balsamic glaze and season with salt and pepper.
4. Serve immediately as a refreshing appetizer.

Herb-Crusted Lamb Chops

Ingredients:

- 8 lamb chops
- 2 tablespoons olive oil
- 1/4 cup fresh rosemary, chopped
- 1/4 cup fresh thyme, chopped
- 3 cloves garlic, minced
- Salt and pepper to taste
- 1 tablespoon Dijon mustard

Instructions:

1. Preheat the oven to 400°F (200°C).
2. In a small bowl, combine rosemary, thyme, garlic, salt, and pepper. Rub the lamb chops with olive oil, then coat with the herb mixture.
3. Heat a skillet over medium-high heat and sear the lamb chops for 2-3 minutes per side.
4. Brush the chops with Dijon mustard and transfer to the oven. Roast for 8-10 minutes for medium-rare, or longer for your desired doneness.
5. Let rest for 5 minutes before serving.

Stuffed Mushrooms with Cream Cheese and Herbs

Ingredients:

- 16 large mushroom caps, stems removed
- 8 oz cream cheese, softened
- 1/4 cup fresh parsley, chopped
- 1/4 cup grated Parmesan cheese
- 1 teaspoon garlic powder
- Salt and pepper to taste
- 1/4 cup breadcrumbs

Instructions:

1. Preheat the oven to 375°F (190°C).
2. In a bowl, combine the cream cheese, parsley, Parmesan, garlic powder, salt, and pepper.
3. Stuff each mushroom cap with the cream cheese mixture and top with breadcrumbs.
4. Arrange the stuffed mushrooms on a baking sheet and bake for 20 minutes, or until golden and bubbly.

Spinach and Ricotta Stuffed Chicken Breast

Ingredients:

- 4 chicken breasts
- 1 cup ricotta cheese
- 1 cup fresh spinach, chopped
- 1/4 cup Parmesan cheese, grated
- 1 teaspoon garlic powder
- Salt and pepper to taste
- 1 tablespoon olive oil

Instructions:

1. Preheat the oven to 375°F (190°C).
2. In a bowl, mix the ricotta, spinach, Parmesan, garlic powder, salt, and pepper.
3. Make a pocket in each chicken breast and stuff with the spinach mixture.
4. Heat olive oil in a skillet and sear the chicken for 3-4 minutes per side.
5. Transfer the chicken to the oven and bake for 15-20 minutes, or until the chicken is cooked through.

Seared Scallops with Citrus Butter Sauce

Ingredients:

- 12 large sea scallops
- 2 tablespoons butter
- 1 tablespoon olive oil
- Salt and pepper to taste
- Juice and zest of 1 orange
- Juice of 1 lemon
- 1 tablespoon fresh parsley, chopped

Instructions:

1. Pat the scallops dry with paper towels and season with salt and pepper.
2. In a large skillet, heat the butter and olive oil over medium-high heat.
3. Add the scallops and sear for 2-3 minutes per side, until golden brown and cooked through.
4. Remove the scallops and set aside.
5. Add the orange juice, lemon juice, and zest to the skillet, stirring to combine. Let simmer for 2-3 minutes.
6. Return the scallops to the skillet and drizzle with the citrus butter sauce.
7. Garnish with fresh parsley and serve.

Roasted Vegetable Medley

Ingredients:

- 1 zucchini, sliced
- 1 bell pepper, chopped
- 1 medium red onion, sliced
- 1 cup cherry tomatoes
- 1 tablespoon olive oil
- Salt and pepper to taste
- 1 teaspoon dried oregano

Instructions:

1. Preheat the oven to 400°F (200°C).
2. Toss the vegetables with olive oil, salt, pepper, and oregano.
3. Spread in a single layer on a baking sheet.
4. Roast for 20-25 minutes, or until tender and lightly browned.

Prosciutto-Wrapped Asparagus

Ingredients:

- 12 asparagus spears, trimmed
- 6 slices prosciutto, halved lengthwise
- Olive oil for drizzling
- Salt and pepper to taste

Instructions:

1. Preheat the oven to 375°F (190°C).
2. Wrap each asparagus spear with a slice of prosciutto.
3. Arrange the wrapped asparagus on a baking sheet, drizzle with olive oil, and season with salt and pepper.
4. Bake for 10-15 minutes, or until the prosciutto is crispy and the asparagus is tender.

Classic Caesar Salad

Ingredients:

- 1 head Romaine lettuce, chopped
- 1/2 cup Caesar dressing
- 1/4 cup grated Parmesan cheese
- 1/2 cup croutons
- Freshly cracked black pepper to taste

Instructions:

1. In a large bowl, toss the chopped Romaine lettuce with Caesar dressing until evenly coated.
2. Add the grated Parmesan cheese and toss again.
3. Top with croutons and freshly cracked black pepper.
4. Serve immediately as a side or appetizer.

Chicken Piccata with Capers

Ingredients:

- 4 boneless, skinless chicken breasts
- Salt and pepper to taste
- 1/2 cup flour
- 2 tablespoons olive oil
- 2 tablespoons butter
- 1/4 cup fresh lemon juice
- 1/2 cup chicken broth
- 1/4 cup capers, drained
- 2 tablespoons fresh parsley, chopped

Instructions:

1. Season the chicken breasts with salt and pepper, then dredge in flour, shaking off the excess.
2. In a large skillet, heat olive oil over medium heat. Cook the chicken for 3-4 minutes per side, until golden brown and cooked through. Remove the chicken from the skillet and set aside.
3. In the same skillet, add butter, lemon juice, and chicken broth. Bring to a simmer and scrape up any browned bits from the pan.
4. Stir in the capers and cook for 1-2 minutes.
5. Return the chicken to the skillet and spoon the sauce over the top.
6. Garnish with fresh parsley and serve.

Roasted Potatoes with Rosemary and Garlic

Ingredients:

- 2 lbs baby potatoes, halved
- 2 tablespoons olive oil
- 3 cloves garlic, minced
- 2 tablespoons fresh rosemary, chopped
- Salt and pepper to taste

Instructions:

1. Preheat the oven to 400°F (200°C).
2. In a large bowl, toss the halved potatoes with olive oil, garlic, rosemary, salt, and pepper.
3. Spread the potatoes in a single layer on a baking sheet.
4. Roast for 25-30 minutes, or until golden brown and tender, stirring once or twice during cooking.
5. Serve warm as a side dish.

Duck Breast with Red Wine Reduction

Ingredients:

- 2 duck breasts
- Salt and pepper to taste
- 1/2 cup red wine
- 1 tablespoon balsamic vinegar
- 1 tablespoon honey
- 1 tablespoon butter

Instructions:

1. Score the skin of the duck breasts in a criss-cross pattern. Season with salt and pepper.
2. In a skillet, cook the duck breasts skin-side down over medium heat for 5-6 minutes, until the skin is crispy. Flip and cook for an additional 3-4 minutes for medium-rare, or longer to your desired doneness.
3. Remove the duck from the skillet and set aside to rest.
4. In the same skillet, add red wine, balsamic vinegar, and honey. Bring to a simmer and reduce by half.
5. Stir in butter until the sauce is smooth.
6. Slice the duck breasts and drizzle with the red wine reduction. Serve immediately.

Mushroom Risotto

Ingredients:

- 1 cup Arborio rice
- 4 cups chicken or vegetable broth
- 1 cup white wine
- 2 tablespoons butter
- 1 tablespoon olive oil
- 1 small onion, chopped
- 2 cups mushrooms, sliced
- 1/2 cup Parmesan cheese, grated
- Salt and pepper to taste
- Fresh parsley, chopped for garnish

Instructions:

1. In a small saucepan, heat the broth over low heat.
2. In a large skillet, heat olive oil and butter over medium heat. Add the onion and cook for 3-4 minutes, until softened.
3. Add the mushrooms and cook for another 5 minutes, until softened.
4. Stir in the rice and cook for 2 minutes, allowing the rice to lightly toast.
5. Add the white wine and cook until absorbed.
6. Gradually add the warm broth, one ladle at a time, stirring constantly, until the rice is tender and creamy (about 20-25 minutes).
7. Stir in the Parmesan cheese and season with salt and pepper.
8. Garnish with fresh parsley and serve.

Seared Tuna with Soy-Maple Glaze

Ingredients:

- 2 tuna steaks
- Salt and pepper to taste
- 1/4 cup soy sauce
- 2 tablespoons maple syrup
- 1 tablespoon rice vinegar
- 1 teaspoon sesame oil
- 1 tablespoon fresh ginger, grated
- 1 tablespoon sesame seeds

Instructions:

1. Season the tuna steaks with salt and pepper.
2. Heat a skillet over high heat and sear the tuna steaks for 1-2 minutes per side, or until the outside is golden brown and the inside remains rare.
3. In a small saucepan, combine soy sauce, maple syrup, rice vinegar, sesame oil, and ginger. Bring to a simmer and cook for 2-3 minutes, until slightly thickened.
4. Drizzle the glaze over the tuna steaks and sprinkle with sesame seeds. Serve immediately.

Roasted Beet and Goat Cheese Salad

Ingredients:

- 3 medium beets, roasted and sliced
- 4 cups mixed greens (arugula, spinach, etc.)
- 1/4 cup goat cheese, crumbled
- 1/4 cup walnuts, toasted
- 2 tablespoons balsamic vinegar
- 1 tablespoon olive oil
- Salt and pepper to taste

Instructions:

1. Roast the beets by wrapping them in foil and baking at 375°F (190°C) for 45-60 minutes. Let cool, peel, and slice.
2. Arrange the mixed greens on a platter. Top with roasted beets, goat cheese, and toasted walnuts.
3. Drizzle with balsamic vinegar and olive oil, then season with salt and pepper.
4. Serve immediately as a light starter or side.

Lobster Bisque

Ingredients:

- 1 lb lobster meat, cooked and chopped
- 2 tablespoons butter
- 1 small onion, chopped
- 2 cloves garlic, minced
- 1/4 cup brandy or sherry
- 3 cups seafood or chicken broth
- 1 cup heavy cream
- 1/2 teaspoon paprika
- Salt and pepper to taste
- Fresh parsley for garnish

Instructions:

1. In a large pot, melt the butter over medium heat. Add the onion and garlic and cook until softened, about 5 minutes.
2. Add the brandy or sherry and cook for 2 minutes, scraping up any bits from the bottom of the pot.
3. Add the broth and bring to a simmer. Cook for 10 minutes.
4. Stir in the lobster meat, heavy cream, paprika, salt, and pepper. Simmer for 5-7 minutes.
5. Use an immersion blender to puree the soup until smooth (or leave it chunky for texture).
6. Garnish with fresh parsley and serve hot.

Parmesan Crusted Tilapia

Ingredients:

- 4 tilapia fillets
- 1/2 cup grated Parmesan cheese
- 1/2 cup panko breadcrumbs
- 1 teaspoon garlic powder
- Salt and pepper to taste
- 2 tablespoons butter, melted
- 1 tablespoon olive oil

Instructions:

1. Preheat the oven to 375°F (190°C).
2. In a shallow dish, combine Parmesan cheese, panko breadcrumbs, garlic powder, salt, and pepper.
3. Brush the tilapia fillets with melted butter and dip into the breadcrumb mixture, pressing to coat.
4. In a skillet, heat olive oil over medium-high heat. Cook the fillets for 2-3 minutes per side until golden brown.
5. Transfer the fillets to a baking sheet and bake for 8-10 minutes, or until the fish flakes easily with a fork.
6. Serve immediately.

Honey-Glazed Carrots with Thyme

Ingredients:

- 4 cups baby carrots
- 2 tablespoons butter
- 2 tablespoons honey
- 1 tablespoon fresh thyme, chopped
- Salt and pepper to taste

Instructions:

1. In a pot, steam or boil the baby carrots until tender, about 10 minutes.
2. In a skillet, melt the butter over medium heat. Stir in the honey and cook for 2 minutes.
3. Add the cooked carrots to the skillet and toss to coat with the honey mixture.
4. Stir in the fresh thyme and season with salt and pepper.
5. Serve immediately as a side dish.

Filet Mignon with Garlic Butter

Ingredients:

- 4 filet mignon steaks
- Salt and pepper to taste
- 2 tablespoons olive oil
- 4 tablespoons butter
- 4 cloves garlic, minced
- 2 sprigs fresh thyme
- 1 tablespoon fresh parsley, chopped

Instructions:

1. Preheat the oven to 400°F (200°C).
2. Season the filet mignon steaks with salt and pepper on both sides.
3. Heat olive oil in a skillet over medium-high heat. Once hot, sear the steaks for 2-3 minutes per side until browned.
4. Add the butter, garlic, and thyme to the skillet. Spoon the melted butter over the steaks as they cook for another 2-3 minutes for medium-rare or longer for desired doneness.
5. Transfer the skillet to the oven and roast for 5-6 minutes (adjust time for your preferred doneness).
6. Remove from the oven and let the steaks rest for 5 minutes.
7. Garnish with fresh parsley and serve.

Grilled Vegetables with Balsamic Glaze

Ingredients:

- 1 zucchini, sliced
- 1 bell pepper, sliced
- 1 eggplant, sliced
- 1 red onion, sliced
- 1/4 cup olive oil
- Salt and pepper to taste
- 1/4 cup balsamic vinegar
- 1 tablespoon honey

Instructions:

1. Preheat the grill to medium-high heat.
2. Toss the sliced vegetables in olive oil, salt, and pepper.
3. Grill the vegetables for 3-4 minutes per side, until tender and charred.
4. In a small saucepan, combine balsamic vinegar and honey. Bring to a simmer and cook for 5-6 minutes until the glaze thickens.
5. Drizzle the balsamic glaze over the grilled vegetables before serving.

Creamy Polenta with Wild Mushrooms

Ingredients:

- 1 cup polenta
- 4 cups vegetable broth
- 1/2 cup heavy cream
- 2 tablespoons butter
- 2 tablespoons Parmesan cheese, grated
- 2 cups wild mushrooms, sliced
- 1 tablespoon olive oil
- 1 clove garlic, minced
- Salt and pepper to taste

Instructions:

1. Bring the vegetable broth to a boil in a medium pot. Slowly whisk in the polenta. Reduce the heat and cook, stirring constantly, for 20-25 minutes until thickened.
2. Stir in the heavy cream, butter, and Parmesan cheese. Season with salt and pepper.
3. In a separate skillet, heat olive oil over medium heat. Add the garlic and wild mushrooms. Sauté for 5-6 minutes until the mushrooms are tender.
4. Spoon the creamy polenta onto plates and top with the sautéed wild mushrooms. Serve immediately.

Shrimp and Grits

Ingredients:

- 1 lb large shrimp, peeled and deveined
- 1 tablespoon olive oil
- 1 tablespoon butter
- 1/2 teaspoon paprika
- Salt and pepper to taste
- 2 cups chicken broth
- 1 cup grits
- 1/2 cup heavy cream
- 1/4 cup cheddar cheese, shredded
- 2 tablespoons fresh parsley, chopped

Instructions:

1. Bring chicken broth to a boil in a medium pot. Slowly whisk in the grits. Reduce the heat and simmer, stirring occasionally, for 20-25 minutes. Stir in the heavy cream and cheddar cheese, then season with salt and pepper.
2. While the grits cook, heat olive oil and butter in a skillet over medium-high heat. Season the shrimp with paprika, salt, and pepper. Sauté the shrimp for 2-3 minutes per side until pink and cooked through.
3. Serve the shrimp over the creamy grits and garnish with fresh parsley.

Grilled Rack of Lamb with Mint Yogurt Sauce

Ingredients:

- 1 rack of lamb, frenched
- 2 tablespoons olive oil
- 2 cloves garlic, minced
- 1 tablespoon fresh rosemary, chopped
- Salt and pepper to taste
- 1/2 cup Greek yogurt
- 2 tablespoons fresh mint, chopped
- 1 tablespoon lemon juice

Instructions:

1. Preheat the grill to medium-high heat.
2. Rub the rack of lamb with olive oil, garlic, rosemary, salt, and pepper.
3. Grill the lamb for 5-6 minutes per side, or until it reaches your preferred level of doneness.
4. While the lamb grills, mix together the Greek yogurt, mint, and lemon juice to make the mint yogurt sauce.
5. Let the lamb rest for 5 minutes before slicing. Serve with the mint yogurt sauce.

Crab Cakes with Lemon Aioli

Ingredients:

- 1 lb lump crab meat
- 1/4 cup breadcrumbs
- 2 tablespoons mayonnaise
- 1 tablespoon Dijon mustard
- 1 egg, beaten
- 1 tablespoon fresh parsley, chopped
- 1 tablespoon lemon juice
- Salt and pepper to taste
- 2 tablespoons olive oil
- 1/4 cup mayonnaise
- 1 tablespoon lemon juice
- 1 teaspoon garlic, minced

Instructions:

1. In a bowl, combine crab meat, breadcrumbs, mayonnaise, mustard, egg, parsley, lemon juice, salt, and pepper. Mix gently.
2. Form the mixture into 6-8 patties.
3. Heat olive oil in a skillet over medium-high heat. Cook the crab cakes for 3-4 minutes per side until golden brown.
4. For the aioli, mix together mayonnaise, lemon juice, and garlic.
5. Serve the crab cakes with lemon aioli.

Roasted Cauliflower with Tahini Sauce

Ingredients:

- 1 head cauliflower, cut into florets
- 2 tablespoons olive oil
- 1 teaspoon cumin
- Salt and pepper to taste
- 1/4 cup tahini
- 2 tablespoons lemon juice
- 1 tablespoon olive oil
- 2 cloves garlic, minced
- 1 tablespoon fresh parsley, chopped

Instructions:

1. Preheat the oven to 400°F (200°C).
2. Toss the cauliflower florets with olive oil, cumin, salt, and pepper. Roast for 20-25 minutes, stirring once or twice until tender and golden brown.
3. For the tahini sauce, whisk together tahini, lemon juice, olive oil, garlic, salt, and pepper until smooth.
4. Drizzle the tahini sauce over the roasted cauliflower and garnish with fresh parsley.

Braised Short Ribs with Mashed Potatoes

Ingredients:

- 4 beef short ribs
- Salt and pepper to taste
- 2 tablespoons olive oil
- 1 onion, chopped
- 2 carrots, chopped
- 2 celery stalks, chopped
- 2 cloves garlic, minced
- 1 bottle red wine
- 2 cups beef broth
- 2 tablespoons fresh thyme
- 2 tablespoons butter
- 4 large potatoes, peeled and diced
- 1/2 cup heavy cream

Instructions:

1. Preheat the oven to 325°F (165°C).
2. Season the short ribs with salt and pepper. Heat olive oil in a large pot over medium-high heat and brown the short ribs on all sides.
3. Remove the ribs and set aside. In the same pot, add onion, carrots, celery, and garlic. Cook until softened, about 5-7 minutes.
4. Add the red wine and beef broth, scraping the bottom of the pot to release any browned bits. Stir in thyme.
5. Return the short ribs to the pot, cover, and braise in the oven for 2.5-3 hours until the meat is tender.
6. For the mashed potatoes, boil the potatoes until tender, then mash with butter, heavy cream, salt, and pepper.
7. Serve the short ribs over the mashed potatoes.

Lemon Herb Roasted Chicken

Ingredients:

- 1 whole chicken (about 4 lbs)
- 2 tablespoons olive oil
- 1 lemon, quartered
- 4 sprigs fresh rosemary
- 4 sprigs fresh thyme
- 4 cloves garlic, smashed
- Salt and pepper to taste

Instructions:

1. Preheat the oven to 425°F (220°C).
2. Pat the chicken dry with paper towels. Rub the chicken with olive oil, salt, and pepper.
3. Stuff the cavity with lemon, rosemary, thyme, and garlic.
4. Roast the chicken for 1 hour 20 minutes, or until the internal temperature reaches 165°F (75°C).
5. Let the chicken rest for 10 minutes before carving and serving.

Ratatouille

Ingredients:

- 1 eggplant, diced
- 1 zucchini, diced
- 1 bell pepper, diced
- 1 onion, chopped
- 2 tomatoes, diced
- 2 cloves garlic, minced
- 1 tablespoon olive oil
- 1 teaspoon fresh thyme
- 1 teaspoon fresh basil, chopped
- Salt and pepper to taste

Instructions:

1. Heat olive oil in a large skillet over medium heat. Add the onion and garlic and sauté until softened, about 5 minutes.
2. Add the bell pepper, zucchini, and eggplant, and cook for another 5-7 minutes, stirring occasionally.
3. Stir in the tomatoes, thyme, basil, salt, and pepper. Reduce heat and simmer for 15-20 minutes, stirring occasionally, until vegetables are tender.
4. Adjust seasoning as needed, and serve warm.

Seared Duck Breast with Cherry Sauce

Ingredients:

- 2 duck breasts, skin-on
- Salt and pepper to taste
- 1 cup fresh or frozen cherries, pitted
- 1/4 cup red wine
- 1 tablespoon honey
- 1 tablespoon balsamic vinegar
- 1 tablespoon butter

Instructions:

1. Preheat the oven to 400°F (200°C).
2. Score the skin of the duck breasts in a criss-cross pattern. Season with salt and pepper.
3. Heat a skillet over medium-high heat. Place the duck breasts, skin-side down, and cook for 5-7 minutes until the skin is golden brown and crispy.
4. Flip the duck breasts and transfer the skillet to the oven. Roast for 6-8 minutes for medium-rare, or longer to your desired doneness.
5. While the duck cooks, prepare the cherry sauce: In a small saucepan, combine cherries, red wine, honey, and balsamic vinegar. Simmer over medium heat for 5-7 minutes until the sauce thickens.
6. Stir in butter to finish the sauce.
7. Rest the duck for 5 minutes before serving with the cherry sauce.

Spaghetti Aglio e Olio

Ingredients:

- 12 oz spaghetti
- 1/4 cup olive oil
- 6 cloves garlic, thinly sliced
- 1/2 teaspoon red pepper flakes
- Salt to taste
- 1/4 cup fresh parsley, chopped
- Grated Parmesan cheese for garnish

Instructions:

1. Cook the spaghetti according to package instructions. Drain, reserving 1/2 cup of pasta cooking water.
2. In a large skillet, heat olive oil over medium heat. Add the garlic and red pepper flakes, and sauté for 1-2 minutes until the garlic is fragrant and lightly golden.
3. Add the cooked pasta to the skillet, tossing to coat. Add reserved pasta water if needed to create a light sauce.
4. Season with salt and stir in fresh parsley.
5. Serve with a sprinkle of grated Parmesan cheese.

Pan-Seared Chicken Thighs with Lemon-Thyme Sauce

Ingredients:

- 4 bone-in, skin-on chicken thighs
- Salt and pepper to taste
- 2 tablespoons olive oil
- 1/2 cup chicken broth
- 2 tablespoons fresh lemon juice
- 1 tablespoon fresh thyme, chopped
- 1 tablespoon butter

Instructions:

1. Season the chicken thighs with salt and pepper.
2. Heat olive oil in a large skillet over medium-high heat. Add the chicken thighs, skin-side down, and cook for 6-7 minutes until golden and crispy.
3. Flip the chicken thighs and cook for another 6-8 minutes until the internal temperature reaches 165°F (75°C).
4. Remove the chicken from the skillet and set aside.
5. In the same skillet, add chicken broth, lemon juice, and thyme. Bring to a simmer, scraping up any browned bits from the pan.
6. Stir in butter to create a smooth sauce.
7. Return the chicken to the skillet and spoon the sauce over the top before serving.

Grilled Swordfish with Mango Salsa

Ingredients:

- 4 swordfish steaks
- Olive oil for brushing
- Salt and pepper to taste
- 1 mango, peeled and diced
- 1/4 red onion, finely diced
- 1/4 cup cilantro, chopped
- 1 tablespoon lime juice
- 1 tablespoon honey

Instructions:

1. Preheat the grill to medium-high heat.
2. Brush the swordfish steaks with olive oil and season with salt and pepper.
3. Grill the swordfish for 4-5 minutes per side until cooked through and easily flakes with a fork.
4. Meanwhile, prepare the mango salsa: In a bowl, combine mango, red onion, cilantro, lime juice, and honey.
5. Serve the grilled swordfish with a generous spoonful of mango salsa on top.

Eggplant Parmesan

Ingredients:

- 2 eggplants, sliced into 1/2-inch rounds
- Salt
- 1 1/2 cups all-purpose flour
- 2 eggs, beaten
- 2 cups breadcrumbs
- 1/2 cup Parmesan cheese, grated
- 2 cups marinara sauce
- 1 1/2 cups mozzarella cheese, shredded
- 2 tablespoons fresh basil, chopped

Instructions:

1. Preheat the oven to 375°F (190°C).
2. Salt the eggplant slices and let them sit for 30 minutes to draw out excess moisture. Rinse and pat dry.
3. Dredge the eggplant slices in flour, dip in beaten eggs, then coat in breadcrumbs mixed with Parmesan cheese.
4. Arrange the breaded eggplant slices on a baking sheet and bake for 20-25 minutes, flipping halfway through, until golden and crispy.
5. In a baking dish, layer the eggplant slices with marinara sauce and mozzarella cheese.
6. Bake for an additional 15-20 minutes until the cheese is melted and bubbly.
7. Garnish with fresh basil and serve.

Stuffed Bell Peppers with Quinoa and Feta

Ingredients:

- 4 bell peppers, tops cut off and seeds removed
- 1 cup quinoa, cooked
- 1 cup feta cheese, crumbled
- 1/4 cup black olives, chopped
- 1/4 cup fresh parsley, chopped
- 1/4 teaspoon cumin
- Salt and pepper to taste
- 1/4 cup olive oil

Instructions:

1. Preheat the oven to 375°F (190°C).
2. In a bowl, combine cooked quinoa, feta, olives, parsley, cumin, salt, and pepper.
3. Stuff the bell peppers with the quinoa mixture.
4. Place the stuffed peppers in a baking dish and drizzle with olive oil.
5. Bake for 25-30 minutes, until the peppers are tender. Serve warm.

Grilled Pork Tenderloin with Apple Chutney

Ingredients:

- 1 pork tenderloin (about 1 lb)
- Salt and pepper to taste
- 2 tablespoons olive oil
- 1 tablespoon fresh thyme, chopped
- 2 apples, peeled and diced
- 1/2 onion, chopped
- 1/4 cup apple cider vinegar
- 1 tablespoon brown sugar
- 1/2 teaspoon ground cinnamon

Instructions:

1. Preheat the grill to medium-high heat.
2. Rub the pork tenderloin with olive oil, thyme, salt, and pepper.
3. Grill the pork for 20-25 minutes, turning occasionally, until the internal temperature reaches 145°F (63°C).
4. While the pork cooks, prepare the apple chutney: In a saucepan, combine apples, onion, apple cider vinegar, brown sugar, and cinnamon. Simmer over low heat for 15-20 minutes until the apples are tender and the sauce thickens.
5. Serve the grilled pork with a spoonful of apple chutney.

Spinach Salad with Berries and Walnuts

Ingredients:

- 4 cups fresh spinach leaves
- 1/2 cup mixed berries (strawberries, blueberries, raspberries)
- 1/4 cup walnuts, toasted
- 1/4 cup crumbled goat cheese
- 2 tablespoons balsamic vinaigrette

Instructions:

1. In a large bowl, toss together the spinach, berries, walnuts, and goat cheese.
2. Drizzle with balsamic vinaigrette and toss to coat.
3. Serve immediately as a light and refreshing side dish.

Braised Lamb Shank with Garlic Mashed Potatoes

Ingredients:

- 2 lamb shanks
- Salt and pepper to taste
- 2 tablespoons olive oil
- 1 onion, chopped
- 2 carrots, chopped
- 3 cloves garlic, minced
- 1 cup red wine
- 2 cups beef broth
- 1 tablespoon fresh rosemary, chopped
- 4 large potatoes, peeled and diced
- 1/2 cup heavy cream
- 2 tablespoons butter

Instructions:

1. Preheat the oven to 325°F (165°C).
2. Season the lamb shanks with salt and pepper. Heat olive oil in a large Dutch oven over medium-high heat. Brown the lamb shanks on all sides.
3. Remove the lamb and set aside. Add onion, carrots, and garlic to the pot, sautéing until softened.
4. Add red wine to deglaze the pot, scraping up browned bits from the bottom. Add beef broth and rosemary, then return the lamb shanks to the pot.
5. Cover and bake for 2.5 to 3 hours, until the lamb is tender and falls off the bone.
6. Meanwhile, cook the potatoes in boiling water until tender. Drain and mash with cream and butter.
7. Serve the braised lamb with garlic mashed potatoes.

Grilled Vegetable and Halloumi Skewers

Ingredients:

- 1 block halloumi cheese, cut into cubes
- 1 red bell pepper, cut into chunks
- 1 zucchini, sliced into rounds
- 1 red onion, cut into chunks
- 1 cup cherry tomatoes
- 2 tablespoons olive oil
- 1 teaspoon dried oregano
- Salt and pepper to taste
- Fresh lemon wedges for serving

Instructions:

1. Preheat the grill or grill pan to medium-high heat.
2. Thread the halloumi cubes, bell pepper, zucchini, onion, and cherry tomatoes onto skewers, alternating the ingredients.
3. Brush the skewers with olive oil and sprinkle with oregano, salt, and pepper.
4. Grill the skewers for 3-4 minutes per side, until the vegetables are tender and slightly charred, and the halloumi is golden brown.
5. Serve with fresh lemon wedges for a burst of brightness.

Pan-Seared Sea Bass with Lemon Caper Sauce

Ingredients:

- 2 sea bass fillets
- 2 tablespoons olive oil
- Salt and pepper to taste
- 2 tablespoons butter
- 1 garlic clove, minced
- 1 tablespoon capers, drained
- 1/4 cup dry white wine
- Juice of 1 lemon
- Fresh parsley, chopped (for garnish)

Instructions:

1. Heat the olive oil in a large skillet over medium-high heat.
2. Season the sea bass fillets with salt and pepper.
3. Place the fillets in the pan, skin-side down, and sear for 4-5 minutes per side, until golden and cooked through.
4. Remove the fillets from the pan and set aside.
5. In the same skillet, melt the butter and sauté the garlic for 1 minute until fragrant.
6. Add the capers, white wine, and lemon juice, and simmer for 2-3 minutes, allowing the sauce to reduce slightly.
7. Pour the sauce over the sea bass fillets and garnish with chopped parsley before serving.

Pappardelle with Wild Mushrooms

Ingredients:

- 12 oz pappardelle pasta
- 2 tablespoons olive oil
- 1 lb mixed wild mushrooms (e.g., shiitake, cremini, chanterelle), sliced
- 2 cloves garlic, minced
- 1/2 cup heavy cream
- 1/4 cup white wine
- Salt and pepper to taste
- Fresh parsley, chopped (for garnish)
- Grated Parmesan cheese (for garnish)

Instructions:

1. Cook the pappardelle pasta according to package instructions. Drain and set aside.
2. In a large skillet, heat olive oil over medium heat. Add the wild mushrooms and sauté for 5-7 minutes, until tender and browned.
3. Add the garlic and cook for 1 minute until fragrant.
4. Pour in the white wine and cook for 2-3 minutes, allowing it to reduce slightly.
5. Stir in the heavy cream and season with salt and pepper. Let the sauce simmer for 3-4 minutes until thickened.
6. Toss the cooked pappardelle pasta with the mushroom sauce and cook for an additional 1-2 minutes, allowing the pasta to soak in the sauce.
7. Garnish with fresh parsley and grated Parmesan cheese before serving.

Roasted Herb-Butter Cornish Hen

Ingredients:

- 2 Cornish hens
- 4 tablespoons unsalted butter, softened
- 2 garlic cloves, minced
- 1 tablespoon fresh rosemary, chopped
- 1 tablespoon fresh thyme, chopped
- 1 teaspoon lemon zest
- Salt and pepper to taste
- 1/2 cup chicken broth

Instructions:

1. Preheat the oven to 400°F (200°C).
2. In a small bowl, mix the softened butter with garlic, rosemary, thyme, lemon zest, salt, and pepper.
3. Gently loosen the skin of the Cornish hens and spread the herb butter under the skin, ensuring even coverage.
4. Place the hens on a roasting pan and pour chicken broth around the base of the hens.
5. Roast for 45-50 minutes, or until the hens reach an internal temperature of 165°F (74°C) and the skin is golden and crispy.
6. Let the hens rest for 5 minutes before serving.

Beetroot Salad with Arugula and Walnuts

Ingredients:

- 2 medium-sized beets, cooked and sliced
- 4 cups arugula
- 1/2 cup walnuts, toasted
- 1/4 cup crumbled goat cheese or feta
- 2 tablespoons olive oil
- 1 tablespoon balsamic vinegar
- Salt and pepper to taste

Instructions:

1. In a large bowl, toss the arugula with olive oil and balsamic vinegar.
2. Add the sliced beets and toss gently to combine.
3. Top the salad with toasted walnuts and crumbled goat cheese or feta.
4. Season with salt and pepper to taste and serve immediately.

Shrimp and Avocado Salad

Ingredients:

- 1 lb cooked shrimp, peeled and deveined
- 2 ripe avocados, diced
- 1 cucumber, diced
- 1 cup cherry tomatoes, halved
- 1/4 red onion, thinly sliced
- 1/4 cup fresh cilantro, chopped
- 2 tbsp olive oil
- 1 tbsp lime juice
- Salt and pepper, to taste
- Optional: crumbled feta cheese or a sprinkle of chili flakes

Instructions:

1. In a large bowl, combine the shrimp, diced avocados, cucumber, tomatoes, and red onion.
2. Drizzle with olive oil and lime juice. Toss gently to combine.
3. Season with salt, pepper, and cilantro. Mix again.
4. Garnish with feta cheese or chili flakes if desired.
5. Serve immediately or chill for 10-15 minutes before serving for a refreshing dish.

Baked Ziti with Fresh Mozzarella

Ingredients:

- 1 lb ziti pasta
- 3 cups marinara sauce
- 2 cups fresh mozzarella, cubed
- 1/2 cup grated Parmesan cheese
- 1 tbsp olive oil
- 1/4 cup fresh basil, chopped
- Salt and pepper, to taste

Instructions:

1. Preheat your oven to 375°F (190°C). Grease a 9x13-inch baking dish with olive oil.
2. Cook the ziti pasta according to package instructions, then drain and set aside.
3. In a large bowl, mix the cooked pasta with marinara sauce, mozzarella, and half of the Parmesan cheese.
4. Season with salt and pepper, then transfer the mixture to the prepared baking dish.
5. Sprinkle the remaining Parmesan cheese on top and cover the dish with aluminum foil.
6. Bake for 25 minutes, then remove the foil and bake for an additional 10 minutes or until the top is golden and bubbly.
7. Garnish with fresh basil before serving.

Grilled Flatbreads with Olive Tapenade

Ingredients:

- 4 flatbreads or naan breads
- 1/2 cup olive tapenade (store-bought or homemade)
- 2 tbsp olive oil
- 1 tsp dried oregano
- Salt and pepper, to taste
- Optional: fresh parsley or basil for garnish

Instructions:

1. Preheat the grill or a grill pan over medium-high heat.
2. Brush both sides of the flatbreads with olive oil and season with oregano, salt, and pepper.
3. Place the flatbreads on the grill and cook for 2-3 minutes per side or until grill marks appear and they are lightly crispy.
4. Remove from the grill and spread a generous amount of olive tapenade on top of each flatbread.
5. Garnish with fresh herbs, if desired, and serve immediately.

Sweet Potato Gnocchi with Sage Butter

Ingredients:

- 2 medium sweet potatoes, peeled and cubed
- 1 1/2 cups all-purpose flour, plus extra for dusting
- 1/2 tsp salt
- 1/4 tsp ground nutmeg
- 1 egg
- 1/4 cup unsalted butter
- 12 fresh sage leaves
- Salt and pepper, to taste

Instructions:

1. Boil the sweet potatoes in a large pot of salted water until tender, about 10-15 minutes. Drain and mash the potatoes until smooth.
2. Allow the mashed sweet potatoes to cool slightly. Add flour, salt, nutmeg, and egg. Mix until a dough forms.
3. On a floured surface, roll the dough into ropes and cut them into bite-sized pieces.
4. Gently press each piece with a fork to create ridges. Bring a large pot of salted water to a boil and cook the gnocchi in batches for 2-3 minutes, or until they float to the surface. Remove with a slotted spoon.
5. In a separate pan, melt butter over medium heat. Add the sage leaves and cook for 1-2 minutes until crispy.
6. Toss the cooked gnocchi in the sage butter, season with salt and pepper, and serve immediately.

Tiramisu with Fresh Berries

Ingredients:

- 1 cup heavy cream
- 1/2 cup mascarpone cheese
- 1/4 cup powdered sugar
- 1 tsp vanilla extract
- 1/2 cup strong brewed coffee, cooled
- 1/4 cup coffee liqueur (optional)
- 24 ladyfinger cookies
- 1 cup mixed fresh berries (strawberries, raspberries, blueberries)
- Cocoa powder, for dusting

Instructions:

1. In a mixing bowl, whip the heavy cream, mascarpone, powdered sugar, and vanilla extract until soft peaks form.
2. In a shallow dish, combine the coffee and coffee liqueur (if using). Briefly dip each ladyfinger into the coffee mixture.
3. Layer the dipped ladyfingers in the bottom of a serving dish.
4. Spread a layer of mascarpone mixture over the ladyfingers. Repeat the layers until all ingredients are used, finishing with a mascarpone layer on top.
5. Refrigerate for at least 4 hours, preferably overnight, to allow the flavors to meld.
6. Before serving, top with fresh berries and dust with cocoa powder.

www.ingramcontent.com/pod-product-compliance
Lightning Source LLC
LaVergne TN
LVHW081503060526
838201LV00056BA/2909